RITUALS
edited by Brina Patel

Rituals

AN ANTHOLOGY OF NONFICTION AND
POETRY EXPLORING THE PRESENCE
AND SIGNIFICANCE OF RITUAL

edited by Brina Patel

bell press
anthologies

ISBN 978-0-9948127-7-3 (print) | ISBN 978-0-9948127-9-7 (ebook)

Edited by Brina Patel
Copyediting by Devon Field
Cover and text design by Angela Caravan

LIBRARY AND ARCHIVES CANADA CATALOGUING IN PUBLICATION
Title: Rituals : an anthology of nonfiction and poetry exploring the presence and significance of
   ritual / edited by Brina Patel.
Other titles: Rituals (2022)
Names: Patel, Brina, editor.
Identifiers: Canadiana (print) 20220455449 | Canadiana (ebook) 2022045566X | ISBN 9780994812773
      (softcover) | ISBN 9781738716708 (Kindle) | ISBN 9780994812797 (EPUB)
Subjects: LCSH: Habit—Literary collections. | LCSH: Manners and customs—Literary collections. |
   LCGFT: Literature.
Classification: LCC PN6071.L6 R58 2022 | DDC 820.8/0355—dc23

Bell Press publishes and operates on the unceded Coast Salish Territories of the Musqueam, Tsleil Waututh, and Squamish people.

Thank you to everyone who supported our Kickstarter to bring this book to life!

Extra special thanks to:

Linda & Mark Pickering
Tobias Toleman
Cathy Caravan

bellpressbooks.com
Twitter: @bellpressbooks
Instagram: @bellpressbooks

Contents

Introduction

RITUALS OFFER US A SOURCE of solace and stability in world of constant flux. Some—basic grooming and sustenance habits—become so habituated we seldom consider them rituals. But others, often those rooted in relationships, culture, religion, or challenging emotions, allow us to break free from autopilot, to pause and reflect on a deeper universal truth.

We've always relied on rituals. But their importance became apparent with the recent Covid-19 pandemic, as many of our lives were upended, forcing us to carve out new ways of rootedness in times of uncertainty. Rituals allowed so many people around the globe to reclaim their control when circumstances no longer offered predictability. They taught us that we are capable of adapting, and allowed us to attach meaning to the mundane.

This collection of poetry and nonfiction explores rituals as they manifest in the lives of a variety of individuals. We have a poem in which the author reflects on her late father, describing the rituals that keep her going after his death. An essay about one author's Sunday testosterone ritual. Another poem about trying to greet a friend at Target while grappling with grief. Each, while unique in its own way, carries a common theme—that in moments of deep strife, of profound precariousness, rituals are the buoy that keep us afloat.

With each piece of prose or poetry, we receive a deeper understanding of rituals and the role they play in this human existence. We begin to question ourselves: How do rituals show up in my life? What have these rituals offered me?

Brina Patel, editor

On the Bound

By Iqra Abid

(after fiona apple)

faith bleeds from the blisters on my
fingers and i don't know who i'm
praying for anymore.

i wonder, is there a limit to the
amount of suffering you can ask
god to resolve? how

many splintered souls can you ask him
to save? most days, it feels like too
much to ask of him

while other days it's not nearly enough.
it turns out religion is just repeating the
same prayers

more than five times a day and
hoping each time they might finally
be heard.

i count on my fingers all the names i can
remember, reciting half-hearted well-wishes
with

a tongue that no longer trusts god. it has
gotten harder to find him in the little things
like i used to.

the mundane has been buried beneath the
pressure of grief and there are no more
miracles buzzing under

my skin. still, each plea slips from the
small of my lips in quiet whispers as i
recall memorized

phrases in a language i cannot
understand. i was taught to bow to an
unseen face, to touch

my forehead to the ground and let faith
wrap itself around my throat; to believe it
when it tells me

that i am loved. time has turned worship
into a habit rather than a practice and i
don't know

who i'm praying to anymore. months go
by and i only call on god for luck; say
bismillah every time

i get into a car or climb onto the bus,
believing it will keep me safe. when i
ask for protection,

recite the 4-qul to ward off evil before i
sleep, it does not feel like a request to an
all-knowing being.

it feels like speaking into the air and
hoping something is listening—possibly
the trees, or the

universe, or its stars, or our beaming
moon, maybe god too. sometimes the
dead visit me

in my dreams and tell me to pray; they ask
me to do more than make feeble requests
and perform

surahs for potential eavesdroppers. they
tell me some faith may do me some
good, and i shrug

in response. i guess it would but to have
faith you need something to believe in and
i'm only ever

on the cusp, on the bound of believing. i
don't think i can ever call god mine if i
can't drown in

the endlessness of sanctity, i am still just
waiting to be tipped over the edge and into
the graces of

divine love.

Iqra Abid (she/her) is a queer Muslim writer based in Canada. Her work focuses on religion, queerness, heritage, mental illness, and intergenerational trauma. She is currently an undergraduate student studying psychology, neuroscience and behaviour. Iqra is also the founder and Editor-in-Chief of *Kiwi Collective Magazine*. Her work can be found in various publications such as *TRAD Magazine*, *Hamilton Review of Books*, *Changing Womxn Collective*, *Crossed Paths Magazine*, and more.

Chance Meeting

by Gabby Gilliam

Not quite strangers find themselves
sharing an aisle at Target, bathed
in fluorescent lights nearly as bright
as their forced smiles.

"How are you?"

flashing teeth ask and I want to say

I spent the night sweat-slick
and shallow-breathed
and my throat constricts
when I practice eulogizing
my father (his funeral is Friday)

but my tongue continues the conversation
clings to rote memory so

"Good, you?"

passes lips before brain
has a chance at honesty.

Our carts glide past each other
and the smiles are tucked away
before we reach the corner
the ritual of feigning contentment
executed flawlessly.

Gabby Gilliam lives in the DC metro area with her husband and son. Her poetry has most recently appeared in *Tofu Ink*, *The Ekphrastic Review*, *Pure Slush*, *Deep Overstock*, *Vermillion*, *MacQueen's Quinterly*, and *Equinox*. You can find her online at gabbygilliam.squarespace.com or on Facebook at facebook.com/GabbyGilliamAuthor.

An Unusual Night

by Livia Meneghin

—*after Sophie Collins' "An Unusual Day"*

If she
wasn't lying awake, she
was shrinking in the fetal position. If she
wasn't shrinking in the fetal position, she
was cracking her knuckles. If she
wasn't cracking her knuckles, she
was grinding her teeth. If she
wasn't grinding her teeth, she
was scrolling for lost words on a screen with blue light. If she
wasn't scrolling for lost words on a screen with blue light, she
was otherwise falling off a cliff in a nightmare. If she
wasn't falling off a cliff in a nightmare, she
was pretending to hold the only soul she
ever kissed. If she
wasn't lying awake, shrinking in the fetal position, cracking
her knuckles, grinding her teeth,

      scrolling for lost words on a screen with blue light,
      falling off a cliff in a nightmare, or pretending to
      hold the only soul she
ever kissed, she

was most likely out enjoying herself. If she
was enjoying herself, it was an unusual night.

Livia Meneghin (she/her) is the author of *Honey in My Hair*
and *GASHER* reviews. She is the winner of *Breakwater Review*'s
2022 Peseroff Prize, a Writers' Room of Boston Fellowship,
and The Academy of American Poets' 2020 University
Prize. Her writing has found homes in *Solstice Lit, Thrush*, and
elsewhere. She is a cancer survivor.

On Sundays, I stab myself.

by Sawyer Patrick

IT'S BETTER THAN DOING IT on Saturday. By delaying it to Sunday, I can procrastinate, just the one day. Put off what is simultaneously annoying and life-giving and legitimately painful, even after all this time. The novelty wore off a long time ago. My enthusiasm has waned—not because I regret it, far from it in that regard—but because it's fiddly, and it just *hurts,* goddammit.

For the first couple of years, they would ask if I was still enthusiastic at my annual checkup. The nurse practitioner phrased it as, "What's your favorite change since starting 'T'?" I didn't know what they were actually asking at the time, just accepted the question at face-value. In retrospect it seems obvious. I told them it was the beard.

It's funny to say I "stab myself" because, technically speaking, I do. With medical-grade sharps, sure, but that still counts. I suspect my old roommate started it, though I can no longer remember. It sounds like something he would say. He's capable of treating everything with humor, and I love him for it.

So on Sundays, I stab myself.

I do it on Sunday—the *Lord's day*—out of spite. Out of the angry and dramatic assertion that I, too, am a sacred thing—even in this form. *Especially* in this form. I was too new to recognize when a wordless and enduring fury started, and am now too old to know what to do with it. It's been four years, a tiny sliver of time for my Elders, but an eon to myself.

It begins, as any good religious ritual does, with cleansing myself. Hand washing, and new paper towel instead of the bathroom hand towel. Then you clean the tiny glass bottle, the size of my pinky. They only hold two doses each, so I have a growing collection I don't know how to respectfully dispose of. Each needle is new, individually packaged for cleanliness and safety, and purchased wholesale online because the pharmacist refused to sell them to me without an "injectable" on file. Even this communion I must scrape and steal and acquire for myself.

Fill the syringe with air, release the air in the bottle. An equal exchange, a fair trade. There's a proper, scientific reason for every step, but there's holiness here too, I choose to believe, even in the most tedious parts. Sometimes the shots draw blood. My shirts and binders have tiny spots over the stomach. Just a drop.

I call the vaccine by the same nickname: getting stabbed. A communal communion. I even got my first dose in the event hall of a church. We move in circles, rotating around what's most important in our lives. I circle God. She circles me. We trade injectables as hundreds or millions die from hate or disease. Or hate *and* disease, some of us; my Elders, living and dying in their own epidemic. A generation of my transgender siblings and queer ancestors who I know only through the symbols and rituals they left behind: the rainbow, the riot.

I wash my hands, cleanse the bottle, draw it out, cleanse myself. I circle my Elders, their memory circles me. I thought of them when the pharmacist turned me away, stealing their own forbidden communion, throwing bricks for the right to simply exist.

I reserve a corner of my already tiny counter for this alone. I try to keep it clean and don't put anything else there. This is my altar, tiny and improvisational as it is, where the transubstantiation happens. Where bread becomes body, female becomes male. Where God visits, greets us with His physical presence. Where my body is created. Not the one the haphazard fray of genetics produced for me, but mine. The one I created for myself, deliberately, with difficulty.

Sometimes I chicken out. I think about it too much. I watch as the needle presses against skin without breaking, and I have to stop and take a deep breath. I reset and try again, letting four years of muscle memory finish what I started. Sometimes I pay too much attention to what I'm doing, and it hurts as it pierces the skin. I'm not afraid of needles but I am afraid of pain.

Nonetheless, I stab myself on Sundays.

Lots of people stab themselves, for lots of different reasons. My aunt was diabetic. She used to let me watch her test her blood sugar—stab wound #1—and then administer the proper amount of insulin—stab wound #2. When I was a kid, and still afraid of needles, she invited me to use the device that pricked her finger (stab wound #1). At first I said no, but agreed a few minutes later. So I got a stab wound and a band-aid of my own for my courage, and it wasn't so bad.

I don't know what she felt about stabbing herself. I never got to talk to her about it, for she passed away the summer before I started. She never got to see this version of me—not on earth, anyway. She did it multiple times a day, something I cannot imagine. She brought her altar with her—a little kit, for her convenience. In fact, her soft encouragement for me to be brave took place at my grandmother's dining room table.

Years later, when I was at my grandmother's and my friend reminded me to stab myself, my grandmother mistook it and thought I was testing my blood sugar.

I think my aunt and I worshiped at the same altar. That same annoying, life-giving, painful altar. I wish I knew what she thought when she bled at it.

I do it Sunday night, after dinner, before bed. I worship under the yellow bathroom light. I shed my blood at the altar, and am altered in return. I come away a changed man.

It *is* holy because I say it is. Because my Elders lived and died for it, in pursuit of it. Because it has required sacrifice. Because it was always meant to be this way for us, when we approach the altar. Because it means something to me, no matter how fiddly or how much I bleed. It is life-giving. It is sacred. It is.

Sawyer Patrick holds bachelors' degrees in computer science and English because he wants to try a little of everything and extra of that, but storytelling is his greatest passion. When not writing nonfiction, he's writing sci-fi, and the answer to *Star Trek or Star Wars* is 'yes.' He lives in the Great Lakes region, on the unceded land of the Potawatomi, Miami, and many other peoples.

Questions

by Alton Melvar M Dapanas

A neighbor's cemented fence cuts through a chunk of the wingspan one-way road. At the corner, a makeshift grill of banana coated with margarine beside one of the neighborhood's sundry stores, a cockpit, a crowd of rickshaw drivers, some barefoot children holding their slippers, street dogs with eczema. Tonight, this street will dim yellow, casting jaundice on concrete. *Did you once bring a lover here and introduce them as your friend?*[1] This is the same road you tread on as your Grindr app is active, as you check *who's nearby*. And as you pick your way, the bulb light from someone else's front porch and streetlight above another's railing. Have you taken your dose of antihypertensives after breakfast? Locate the rural within the urbansphere, urged the ecocritics. Google Weather says 39 degrees Celsius will peak at noon just in time for your lunch break. But it always rains before nightfall. The weather bureau declares La Niña. Last night, on the island where I live, lightning bellowed over a southern mountain. It afforded the landscape a blink of daylight. Are you still afraid of thunder? The midday sun here, too, is harsh. They warned us of heat stroke.

Hypertension runs in my family, too. And so does schizophrenia. I tell my shrink about you. He nods and jots down a string of words in his notepad. Is this a new template for some therapy meme? A sling bag on your hunched right shoulder, uncertain. Strolling along a busy street—either RN Abejuela Street or Corrales Avenue—but actually dreaming of sitting by a lakeside house like in a movie or a long overdue mountaineering trip. The mayor boasts of the statistics like a messiah. He mentions vaccination rate and number of deaths repeatedly, proud like a coach, as if he alone has made this possible. Is it now safe for hookups? I think I saw you once in a photo on alter Twitter, behind someone else, him covering his face with his phone, and you covering yours with your right hand, your left anchored at the back of his hips. Both of you fronting a mirror. I had a hard-on. In another city, I pass by a mosque on the left, a warehouse of canned meat on the right. Further, a factory of junk food, a subdivision of unfinished housing units. *I thought I saw you at the bus stop. I didn't though.*[2] Half-naked boys gather at one of the road's six lanes. This was on the day Adele released a song after six long years. In another lifetime, I will turn out to be a revenant. *Much can never be redeemed.*[3] My malaise of a chest returns as a gap of mistakes.

1 *You meet some woman on the internet and take her home.* From Taylor Swift's "the 1"

2 Also from Taylor Swift's "the 1"

3 From Mary Oliver's "Don't Hesitate"

Alton Melvar M Dapanas (they/them), a native of southern Philippines, is the author of *Towards a Theory on City Boys* (UK: Newcomer Press, 2021). Published in Sweden, Lebanon, Germany, Taiwan, Ireland, Nigeria, Austria, Japan, South Africa, and the Netherlands, their latest works are in *Modern Poetry in Translation* (UK), *The Best Asian Poetry* (Singapore), *Mekong Review* (Australia), *Baest: A Journal of Queer Forms and Affects* (US), *Canthius Magazine* (Canada), and *Poetry Lab Shanghai* (China) where they were translated into Chinese. They are editor-at-large at *Asymptote Journal*, assistant nonfiction editor at *Panorama: The Journal of Intelligent Travel* and *Atlas & Alice Literary Magazine*, and reader at *Creative Nonfiction* magazine. Find more at linktr.ee/samdapanas.

Coping—in Threes

by Em Walling

I.

She stocks.

> Blossom-scented soaps
> two-in-one shampoos
> plastic shavers
> canned soups
> sauces
> frozen meat from the butcher
> cheap toilet paper
> and napkins.

The kitchen pantry is always full—
yet there's always space for more. If the shelves had knees,
they would buckle forever. She stocks
out of fear of running out. If you ask her
why she is always stocked, she'll tell you
she remembers what it was like as a child to do without—
to know an empty dinner table
when the car breaks down. She vows
to not live that way again. Therefore,
the shelves are stocked.

II.

She lists.

She maintains an active toiletry list on the fridge.

A grocery list on the magnetic to-do calendar—also on
        the fridge.

She uses an app to keep multiple lists. At work, her
        desk transmutes

into a colorful mess of sticky notes full of tasks to complete.

She has lists

        saved on her computer

        websites to update

        homework to finish for grad school.

She fears forgetfulness. A time when she was trying
        to accomplish

so much but always forgot one thing—

like to submit a job application when she was jobless after
        college. So,

she lists.

III.

He plays.

Board games, takes pictures of the boards. Difficult,
        mind-bending,

strategic board games. And he will only play them

on the kitchen table, even though he has the option

to use other spare tables.

He removes

        place mats

        half-empty salt and pepper shakers

        napkins

        glass-blown decorations

        and everything else from the kitchen table.

The game will stay out for days. He works his way through
the terrain, strategizing how to cross a historical front—
and documents the entire activity. He takes comfort
in planning a process and uses this method
to get over the wall and through to the next day. So,
he plays board games.

Em Walling's visual and written work focuses on the physical,
emotional, and psychological connections people have with the
environment. Her writing can be found in numerous journals,
plus poetry anthologies from Shabda Press, University of Hell
Press, and Splintered Disorder Press. She lives in Australia
and volunteers at a seabird rescue organization.

Solitude in the Modern Era

by Sarah E. Azizi

Everyone's got something
smart or smarmy to say.
Much of it is too long-winded
or poorly paragraphed for my liking,
& I'm trying to practice quiet. I take
my waking slow, & slower still, light
incense & candles, play wordless music—
percussion & flutes, a single violin string
reverberating, Middle C held till it fades out.
I held my father's hand as he died. His hand,
soft as a pillow, couldn't grip my palm back.
His eyes & mouth stretched open;
some semblance of him scurried
& fluttered through his protruding
rib cage, then relented, trapped
as it was inside his hollowing body.
The smell of death is at first
the smell of nothing. I was in the preface
of my life at fifteen, desperate to escape
the confines of youth, he the age I am today.
His body lingers in that bed, in my memory,

in the house my mother had to sell
a handful of years later. I inherited his keen
sense of smell, almost disturbingly sensitive.
Crayons made him nauseous, the scent
of impending snow, anxious. But how full
our home would be w/ the scent
of Persian stews simmering: lamb
& eggplant, chickpea & dill. I love a musky
floral, roasted vegetables full of garlic,
fresh linens spritzed w/ rose water
& lavender. I buy rosewater
at the middle eastern grocery, pour
it into spray bottles I pick up at the dollar store,
though of course these days I go out less & less,
& the mental list of keys, wallet, cigarettes,
lighter, chapstick includes *mask*, & probably
always will. The whole world changed
but so much seems the same—death's grand trick,
after all, is whisking the tablecloth off & putting
the setting back almost as it was. I miss so
many people. I go on. Sometimes I use up
hours w/o thinking of anyone I love
who's died. At night, I put the kettle on,
inhale & sip herbs & flowers, rinse my cup,
make sure the lights are shut off. Little
rituals protect my willingness to stay
in the world, cracked as it may be. I cover
myself w/ pink sheets, rustle my feet, sink
into slumber, all the while held by gravity
& the absurd but necessary belief
that something good—
something better—
could happen next.

Sarah E. Azizi (aka Sera Miles) is a queer Iranian-American writer, educator, and activist. Previous and forthcoming publications include *$pread Magazine, Phoebe: An Interdisciplinary Journal of Feminist Scholarship, 34th Parallel, Blue Mesa Review, Fahmidan Journal, Clean Sheets, red, The Tide Rises, HELD, Wrongdoing Magazine, the winnow, Superpresent, Nine Mile, The Coop*, and *Free State Review*. She lives in Albuquerque, New Mexico with her daughter & amongst friends, frenemies, and family of choice.

The Taste of Peppermint

by Kim Bannerman

MY AFTERNOON CUP OF TEA sparks a longing for closure I can never have, for knowledge I can never know.

Why today, of all days, should I remember my college roommate from decades ago? Is it the cup I've used that sparked this memory? Or the way the sunlight catches the amber liquid, speckled with swirling bits of dried leaves? Why am I standing inert in the center of the kitchen, staring down into wreaths of steam, wondering where she's gone?

The last time I saw Faith, I was lying in bed; my memory of her is horizontal and bisected by the narrow aperture of my bedroom door. The school year had finished. It was the last day in our cramped apartment, and she planned to leave at dawn to start the exhausting 12-hour drive back to her hometown. We planned to room together next September and I, being very lazy, didn't get up to see her go. Instead, I waved to her from my mattress as we swapped promises to see each other soon.

That was more than two decades ago.

I wonder how she is. I wonder where she's living. Is she happy? Did she manage to snag a sexy rich cowboy like she'd planned? Faith was one of those people who effortlessly radiated joy. She possessed a wicked sense of humor, a shameless fondness for *Star Trek*, and a wit devoid of all moisture.

Our friendship had been a natural thing, seemingly predetermined. We met in the dorms and, when we'd tired of first-semester shenanigans, we decided to move together to a cheap, ant-infested, third floor apartment, a few blocks off campus—barely a step up in accommodation, but it was ours alone and we cherished the freedom. With its orange shag carpet, lemon-yellow walls, and mid-70s amber swag lamp, the apartment was like living in the center of the sun, so she balanced out the yellow with lots of green house-plants: succulents, an ivy, a potted fern. The neighbors across the hall were some form of drug royalty—maybe not 'lords,' but at least 'barons.' The neighbors next door engaged in a biweekly ménage-a-trois, and as their bedroom shared a wall with Faith's room, we'd sit on her bed and listen to their sexploits, eating popcorn and silently cheering them on. Our little balcony overlooked an empty, weed-choked pool, but the pathetic view and rank stench didn't bother us too much because just beyond the complex lay a vast wildlife sanctuary. We'd take long walks through the wetlands and sit at the top of the birdwatching tower, and speculate about all the grand things we planned to do with our limitless futures.

Every night we ate tuna casserole, and every afternoon we drank peppermint tea, and suddenly I'm flooded with the memory of our brown teapot. Ah! Here is the root of my reminiscing! I glance at the cup in my hand and breathe in its fragrance. My memories roll back to a single night and I start to laugh. Hot tea sloshes, burning my fingers, but I don't care.

One afternoon, I came home from college, threw my books on the couch, and shambled into the kitchen for sustenance. Faith was busy with laundry, so I boiled the kettle and made a pot of tea. When she finished, she joined me in the living room, and we drank tea while watching *Star Trek: TNG*.

It wasn't until the credits started that Faith turned to me, her face grey with anxiety.

"What's wrong?" I said.

"You washed out the teapot, right?"

"No." I said, "Why?"

Horror crossed her features. "I fed the plants," she whispered, "The teapot was half full of plant food. We just drank a whole bunch of fertilizer."

In a flurry, we called Poison Control. I tearfully told the nurse what we'd done, and she assured us we wouldn't die, we'd just feel 'a little green in the morning.' Then she broke into snorts of laughter and gave us a single, poignant instruction: drink as much milk as you can, as fast as possible, to neutralize the nitrogen in the plant food. Then, she added with another giggle, prepare to fart and belch *a lot* over the next 24 hours. Faith and I rushed to the nearest 7-11 to buy out their stock. We spent the night feeling woozy and foolish and bloated, tooting like bassoons.

Peppermint tea. The taste held sunshine, silly blunders, friendships forged in ridiculous mistakes and afternoon rituals. I took a sip and rolled it over my tongue.

Despite the poisoning, Faith was the best roommate I ever had. We never fought, we shared groceries without strife, we even agreed on the housecleaning schedule. We made a pact to use the brown teapot for nothing but glorious tea. We had the same taste in foreign films, we read each other's books, we both enjoyed sharing a beer at the local biker bar after exams. We disbanded our comfortable little nest with every intention of sharing a place the following school year, but life got in the way. Mistakes were made. Paths diverged. Neither one of us returned to school in September, and while we wrote letters for a while, eventually the letters stopped.

I have only a few photos of Faith, but I still enjoy a cup of tea every afternoon. I realize now as I stand here in my kitchen, that singular habit was cemented into my daily routine during our fleeting time together. I drink tea in the afternoon because of her.

Thus, she remains with me, even now as I sip my tea—not in body, of course, but in spirit and intention. I don't know where she's gone, I hate the fact that I've lost touch with her, but the taste of peppermint revives that same joy she brought into every room. I hope, wherever Faith is, she's still the same vibrant, adventurous maverick who made my first years at college so fun.

One more sip. One more sweet, innocent taste of peppermint. I wonder if she thinks of me whenever she feeds her plants. I wonder if she misses me as much as I miss her.

Kim Bannerman writes novels, screenplays, articles and short stories from her home on Vancouver Island, Canada. Her work has appeared in anthologies like *She's Shameless* from St. Martin's Press, *In the Company of Animals* from Nimbus Press, and *When Birds Are Near* from Cornell University Press. She is the author of twelve novels, including the modern fairytale *The Tattooed Wolf*, the historical mystery *Bucket of Blood*, and the Circus Salmagundi Mysteries series. For more information, visit kbannerman.com.

at the end of May

by Stephanie Sesic

for Uvalde

the forest floods with blossoms
phlox purpling the new green like delicate bruises
sweet scratch of honeysuckle
plucked and bitten on the tongue

spring means storm-ready skies
hail like bullets could assault us at any time
blasting apart the unripened fruit
a slick of carnage on the ground

please tell me
that my metaphor is profane
that violence is not a sacrament
we treat it like a force of nature
but name a ritual we perform more often
than wounding

Stephanie Sesic teaches writing at Cuyahoga Community College and is happiest when hiking in the Cuyahoga Valley. Her work has appeared recently in *Sunlight Press, Coastal Shelf, Claw & Blossom,* and *Parks & Points & Poetry.* Her chapbook, *The Intimate Verge*, was published by Pudding House Publications in 2008.

Once Upon A Birthday

by Milton Jordan

That morning in March two office mates
tied black balloons to our doorknob and placed
their sympathy card edged in black crepe
over Thursday on the calendar pad
covering my desk and sat innocently
feigning work at their own as I entered
slowed by their elevator accomplice
and running ten minutes behind schedule.

Now gone years, and miles removed from that work
I reread the order of service Zellars's
younger daughter sent from St. Theresa's
listing Hartman and his accomplice
as honorary pallbearers and know
she will not expect me to reply.

Milton Jordan lives with Anne in Georgetown, Texas. His collection, *A Forest for the Trees*, is forthcoming from Backroom Window Press. He is editing an anthology of poems from the first year of *Texas Poetry Assignment* for Kallisto Gaia Press.

Do This in Remembrance of Me

by Julie Fleming Wickham

I SAT IN THE OVERSTUFFED brown leather recliner and watched Dad lurch around our family room. Marva followed close behind, one hand always on his arm or shoulder or waist, ready to steady him if he stumbled. Six years after his Alzheimer's diagnosis and eight after I started seeing what turned out to be signs of dementia, Dad was mostly silent this day, restless, in his own world, moving around the house and rifling through anything that caught his attention. He'd been up and roaming for nearly 24 hours. Dad was dressed as usual in a white T-shirt and swim trunks, barefoot. His recent agitation-driven habit of rubbing his scalp had left his wavy, white hair in disarray. I observed his gaunt face, the inner stretch of his eyebrows raised, his mouth hanging slack. Dad was lost somewhere I couldn't reach.

Marva, Dad's primary caregiver, had moved from Maryland to Atlanta to care for him. She'd promised to stay for six months, but she supported and loved Dad for nearly 33 months, for the rest of his life. Her sunny personality and good-spirited teasing comforted us both. On this day, though, Marva was exhausted from trying to keep up with him. Her brain, unlike Dad's, demanded rest.

Daphne's friendly *Hello, all!* broke our anxiety-tinged energy as she walked into the family room. I'd been looking forward to her visit all day, eager for the lighter mood she would bring. Daphne and I had met years earlier in church, and she reached out to me soon after Dad's diagnosis to offer support. She understood what we were facing thanks to her experience with her mother's Alzheimer's. Our friendship grew over the many conversations that followed. Dad and I became homebound after a few years: he couldn't leave the house, and I wouldn't leave him. Daphne recognized our isolation and started visiting on Thursday evenings, bringing friendship, empathy, and communion.

Daphne set down a large basket that I knew contained grape juice, bread, and a blue earthenware plate and matching pitcher and chalice. She pulled the loaf of bread out of her basket and handed it to me, saying *I found the rosemary bread this week! Rosemary for remembrance.* Wishing that rosemary could have the power to rekindle Dad's memory, I hurried to the kitchen to warm the loaf in the oven. When I returned, Daphne was sitting in the other recliner chatting with Marva and trying, without success, to engage Dad. He seemed to be searching for something as he circled the room, but we'd learned not to ask what he was hunting for. When he was in his own world, that kind of question might bring him back to our world, but he would rage or cry because he didn't know or couldn't say what he wanted. I was careful not to voice any of the painful emotions I was feeling in front of Dad, but Daphne's warm eyes and quick smile told me she understood the grief, fear, and frustration. We chatted about her work, the book she was writing, news from church—ordinary conversation that felt extraordinary because it was so rare in my life by that time.

As the scent of rosemary wafted from the kitchen into the family room, Dad busied himself going through a stack of junk mail I'd left on a side table for him. He carefully examined each piece of mail, set it aside, and moved to the next. Marva tried to get him to sit; he'd been standing so long that his calves, ankles, and feet were grotesquely swollen and discolored to a deep shade of purple that no human limb should be. Even though he was unsteady, even though I could tell from his haggard expression that he was tired, Dad just moved to another part of the room each time Marva suggested he sit.

I looked away from Dad back to Daphne. She nodded with empathy and encouragement, her blue eyes tender and wistful as she said, *Shall we?* She stood and moved to the corner where she'd left her basket as I pulled an ottoman between and slightly in front of the pair of leather recliners and placed a flat piece of wood on top of it. Daphne laid a cloth with hunter green and burgundy squares across the wood, then filled the pitcher with grape juice and placed it and the chalice on the cloth. I lit a candle and placed it in front of the pitcher while Daphne retrieved the warm rosemary bread. She put the bread on the stoneware plate she'd brought, then set the plate in front of the chalice.

Dad noticed our activity. He stood still and stared at the set table. He ran his right hand through his hair, but more slowly than before, smoothing it into place. I wondered if his agitation might be lifting and hoped that it was, that he wouldn't interrupt communion. I immediately felt shame for wanting peace for the ritual that we were about to begin. All are welcome at this table, I reminded myself, maybe someone who felt lost most of all.

JD, Daphne called, *would you join us for communion?*

Dad continued to stare for another moment, then wobbled to one of the leather recliners. Marva stood in front of him and placed her arms under his, gently lowering him to the seat. Daphne kneeled on the floor next to the table, Marva sat in the other recliner, and I perched on a chair I'd pulled next to Daphne. Our little circle was completed when my English Mastiff Gracie sat next to me, gazing longingly at the bread with her nose twitching. The room settled, so quiet that I could hear cars whizzing by our house.

Daphne prayed over the communion elements, her soft voice giving thanks for our time together, for Dad, for the love and care that Marva and I showed him, for this time to remember Christ's love. I peeked at Dad and saw that his eyes were closed and his head bowed. After we women said *Amen*, Daphne broke the loaf of bread in half and recited the words of institution: *On the night when Jesus was betrayed, He took the bread, and when He had given thanks, He broke it and said…*

My voice joined Daphne's to continue the traditional words: *This is my body, which is for you. Do this in remembrance of me.* As I spoke, I glanced at Dad. He was silent, but his lips were moving.

Daphne poured grape juice from the pitcher into the chalice and continued the liturgy as she lifted the chalice: *In the same way also the cup after supper, saying…*

She and I responded: *This cup is the new covenant in my blood. Do this as often as you drink it, in remembrance of me.* Again, I watched as Dad moved his lips without making a sound. I held my breath, afraid of pulling him out of this moment.

Dad watched intently as Daphne held out the bread and the chalice to me. I broke off a piece of bread and dipped it in the grape juice, then passed the juice-soaked bread to Dad. His hands shook as he placed it into his mouth, chewed, and swallowed. Daphne served Marva and then me, and I held the elements as Daphne pulled and dipped her bread. Finally, Daphne smiled as she tore one more bite of bread from the loaf and gave it to Gracie, who was still sitting patiently in our circle. We laughed as Gracie gulped it down without even chewing; Dad was still silent, fully present at Christ's table.

Daphne closed our communion service with the final words, *For as often as you eat this bread and drink the cup, you proclaim the Lord's death until He comes.* Dad remained calm and attentive. I didn't want to move, and Daphne and Marva both stayed still as peace abided among us. Even Gracie hesitated for a moment before lying down and shaking her head, calling attention to the fact that we still had warm bread sitting on the table. The sound of her long ears flopping and the tags on her collar jingling as she shook her head broke the spell, and we women chuckled. Dad gazed at his hands folded in his lap and sat serenely, unmoving.

Anybody want more? Daphne held out the plate and Marva and I nodded eagerly. Marva bounced up from the chair and moved toward the kitchen as she called, *I'll get the butter!* She paused and turned to Daphne as she asked, *Is that ok? To finish the communion bread with butter?* Daphne laughed and said, *Ok? It's perfect!*

Daphne lifted the remainder of the half-loaf that we'd pulled our communion bread from and held it out to Dad. He took the whole chunk, eagerly biting into it. Marva asked, *Do you want butter, JD?* but Dad kept eating, unwilling to hand over the still-warm bread. Daphne divided the other half-loaf into three pieces, and she, Marva, and I slathered on the butter and ate, each sharing a bit of our bread with Gracie. We turned to light-hearted conversation. I don't remember what we talked about, only that we tried to include Dad and that he smiled and laughed along with us, his face brighter than it had been all day. Soon after we finished communion, Marva took Dad to his bedroom, where he finally fell into a deep sleep.

Looking back, I realize that Dad's participation was about more than years of repetition, more than recognition. We'd sung *Happy Birthday* any number of times; no reaction. He rarely responded to photos of my mother even though they were happily married for nearly 40 years. He lost the ability to use the TV remote, the telephone, sometimes even a knife and fork. Repetition and recognition only carried him so far. Communion called on something else.

I've long believed that dementia is like an opaque pane of glass that occasionally, randomly, cleared enough for us to see and connect with one another. Daphne's invitation to communion and recitation of words that Dad had heard and said for so many years reached through that opaque glass and connected him with the holy. The bread tasted good, sure, but I wonder if he gobbled down the chunk Daphne handed him after communion hoping to take the gifts of communion deeply into himself, to feast on the Spirit that he connected with thanks to the ritual. Dad could remember almost nothing, but he never hesitated as he took the bread and the cup in remembrance of Christ. The sacred touched his soul, and his soul shined through dementia. Amen indeed.

Julie Fleming Wickham moved from her native Atlanta to Cheyenne, Wyoming, after caring for her father (her last living family member) through seven years of dementia. She now writes about thriving after significant loss, Wyoming history and adventures, and dementia. Julie founded The Purple Sherpa, a 501(c)(3) nonprofit organization that educates and encourages dementia family caregivers and consults with attorneys on building their practices. Julie is the author of *The Reluctant Rainmaker: A Guide for Lawyers Who Hate Selling* and *Legal Rainmaking Myths: What You Think You Know About Business Development Can Kill Your Practice*, as well as numerous articles. Learn more at JulieFlemingWickham.com.

Archival Hours

by Angela Acosta

Queer liberation is the work of generations
crying out on the streets and in hospital beds.
I reach for lives at the source,
sifting through diary entries and manuscripts.
I squint at the tight Spanish penmanship,
looking for love and companionship.

If it's just research, then why am I
craning my neck
over books filled with gender theories,
only to find manuscripts covered in battered words
of cancer diagnoses, Alzheimer's, and death
for my beloved writers?

I may be a century too late,
too much of a May-December relationship,
but I've already fallen in love with
these epistolary personalities from Spain
that show the beauty of all that is
handwritten.

Angela Acosta (she/her) is a bilingual Latina poet and scholar from Florida. She won the 2015 Rhina P. Espaillat Award from West Chester University, and her poems have appeared in *Panochazine*, *Olit*, *Heartland Women Writers*, and *Latinx Audio Lit Mag*. She is currently completing her Ph.D. in Iberian Studies at The Ohio State University where she studies the lives and works of early twentieth-century Spanish women writers.

Sing for your Supper

by Paula Rudnick

In Homer's time the outside world
was not a finger tap away.
Beyond one's walls lay wonder,
worth defying Fates to voyage
from the place called home.
Travelers marshalled horses, chariots, boats with oars,
men to row, skins of wine to quiet fear on churning seas.
Strangers landing on a foreign shore
were welcomed with exuberance,
meat and drink laid out unsparingly,
fresh clothes offered after perfumed bath.
Not till every creature comfort was
provided did the host inquire:
Who are you? What's your quest? Tell us your story.

We want a prenup now
before we pour the Chardonnay,
collateral for every borrowed cloak.
Not that friends came easier to Odysseus,
caught between a rock and hard place,
lured to self-destruction by an earworm's purr,
just that tea leaves had more weight
when facts weren't free on Wikipedia.

Who knew when a grateful traveler
might return a kind host's favor,
share a god connection or their knowledge of the stars?
Not to mention gold, whose value stands
the test of time, just like a well-told tale.
Who are you? What's your story? We still want to know.

Paula Rudnick is a former TV producer whose credits range from late night rock and roll to Emmy-nominated movies. She is a political activist and has served on numerous non-profit boards. Her poems have been published in *Halfway Down the Stairs*, *LA Jewish Journal* and *Kosmos Quarterly* as well as in anthologies by Darkhouse Books, Truth Serum Press and Constellations. Her first solo collection *Now is Not a Good Time* was released this spring. Paula has two grown daughters and lives in Los Angeles.

At the Ithaca Farmers Market

by Jane Rosenberg LaForge

I tried to buy some plants for my budding
scientist of a daughter. Colocasia,
she called them. Elephant Ears, when
I was growing up. Poisonous to the mere
touch of children, I read much later,
though my father installed them
along the front of our house. Perhaps
he meant them as a palatial gateway
for the white stucco of our walls amid
adobe and downsized Spanish mansions.
They provided shade and intrigue, layers
of bark that seemed to sprout eyes where
years and branches had been, in a pattern
of hands over fists, the slap happy game
my father would play too hard with us.
My sister never forgave him. The menace
was not in his expression, but the strength
he could not spare; and in the number
of seasons left in the woody record,
too high for my understanding.
Because of Elephant Ears, I thought

I had a special affinity for the tropics,
my grandfather having contracted
malaria. At the kitchen window, my mother
and grandmother bemoaned the closeness
of the weather though we lived in a desert.
But should we experience it, like speaking
in dreams without the use of the mouth,
because in dreams you are omniscient,
aware of all your ancestors, antagonists,
heroes who never get their moment,
it would be under those leaves, alien
and glamorous. I realize in context
I am content with brief flashes when
my daughter engages with my present.
She said no to my offer, because Elephant Ears
always die in winter. Wait until
I go to graduate school, she said,
and move to a more forgiving climate.

Jane Rosenberg LaForge is the author of a memoir,
two novels, three full-length collections of poetry, and four
chapbooks. Her most recent book of poems is *Medusa's
Daughter* (Animal Heart Press 2021), and her most recent book
of prose, a novel, is *Sisterhood of the Infamous* (New Meridian
Arts Press 2021). More work has appeared or is forthcoming in
Pirene's Fountain, Evening Street Review, Panoplyzine, and *Schuylkill
Valley Journal.*

Phases of Recovery from an Eating Disorder

by Summer A.H. Christiansen

Trigger warning: eating disorder thoughts and behaviors

Phase 1:
I Don't Think I Have A Problem.

I SCROLL THROUGH THE ENDLESS pages of #thinspo on Tumblr from under the covers of my bed. I am eighteen years old. My phone screen is filled with pictures of women in skin-tight jeans with inch-wide gaps between their thighs. Young women scantily clad in bikinis with their hip bones showing, still managing to be feminine with waists and breasts and curves in all the right places.

I go to the search bar and type in, "weight loss tips." My goal has been to get down to 120 pounds, but the further I go down the scale, the more I want to lose. 130 becomes 120, which becomes 118, which becomes 115. Maybe, if I try hard enough, I could get down to 110. I think of these women as I skim through the tips.

Drink water instead of eating to fill your hunger.

Do as much cardio as you can. Do not lift weights.

Stop eating sugar.

Do not let junk food touch your lips.

Weight loss motivational quotes are scattered throughout these tips.

A minute on the lips is a lifetime on the hips.

Nothing tastes as good as skinny feels.

When you eat crap, you look like crap.

Don't listen to your inner fat girl. She's unattractive and mean.

This thin-spiration fuels my motivation to shrink. My stomach growls in the quiet of the night. I think of the breakfast I'll make for myself in the morning. My mouth salivates at the thought of one pan-fried egg, one low-fat vanilla bean yogurt with just a sprinkle of cinnamon on it, and maybe a couple of strawberries. If I'm feeling extra hungry and I feel that I've been good enough, I might have half a slice of toast with a bit of butter.

As I fall asleep, I let my mind wander to the images of the thin women and wonder if I'll ever look like that.

Phase 2:
I Might Have A Problem But It's Not That Bad.

There's a point in your weight loss journey where people start to notice the changes in your body and verbalize their feelings on the matter. Their words, both positive and negative, fuel your weight loss.

There's your mentor teacher in your university program who notices when you return from summer break. "Dang girl! You look great!"

There's the doctor at the family clinic that tells you to avoid losing any more weight when you go to get birth control. "It would be unhealthy."

The cousin you never talk to who finally comments on your Instagram photo. "You're sooooo tiny!"

The barista who bullied you in high school tells you that you look so healthy, so skinny. "You look amazing," they say, smiling, as they give back your debit card with their slender, manicured hands.

During finals, you stay up too late, drink too much coffee, don't eat enough food. You stop by your part-time job on campus to print something before you head to class.

"You know it's okay to eat?" your ex-boyfriend comments. You laugh and smile. You're thankful he's noticing you.

Your fiancé's mother cracks jokes about how you're a "skinny bitch." She is wafer-thin herself. It feels like getting a gold star from an expert.

Phase 3:
I Have A Problem But I Don't Care.

A short list of places I've purged:
- A laundromat bathroom
- The bathroom at my barista job
- The bathroom at my teaching job
- The bathroom in my mother's condominium
- The bathroom at my father's house
  - o [bonus points: managing to be quiet while doing so]
- A dirty stall at my first teaching job in South Korea
- The bathroom in my first apartment in South Korea
- In a fancy Japanese toilet in Fukuoka, Japan
- A bathroom outside a Korean BBQ restaurant

Phase 4:
I Want To Change But I Don't Know How
And I'm Scared.

It's early fall in Seoul, South Korea, and the air inside the subway station is warm and sticky. The muted pastel colors of the tiles on the floor and wall remind me of the '80s movies my dad showed me as a child. I've just turned twenty and have moved to South Korea in an attempt to start my life fresh. After a month of trying to find my way, I meet a handsome Canadian man and we start dating. There is something about him that allows me to open up completely. Maybe it's the fact that we're both black sheep, making our own paths across the sea from our families. Maybe it's the fact that he is gentle and kind and listens to me.

Since moving overseas, I've started to throw up more. The women around me are smaller. My Korean co-teacher's thigh is as big as my forearm. I seem like a giant in comparison. The advertisements in the bathroom stalls are for diet pills or plastic surgery and have mirrors attached to them so you can stare at your stomach while you sit down to pee. Everything in my life feels new and out of control.

After almost every meal, I drink extra water to help the food come up easier. I make my way to the bathroom as fast as I possibly can and lower myself towards the bowl of the toilet. I shove the unbristled end of a toothbrush down my throat and keep trying until the food comes up. I throw up until I can't take it anymore or until someone enters the bathroom. I wash or wipe my face. I let the water run over the end of the toothbrush and then brush my teeth vigorously, attempting to get rid of any smell. Sometimes I need to reapply makeup, sometimes I'm okay.

But on this day, after Michael and I have traveled into the heart of Seoul to visit new restaurants, see new sites, I'm tired of hiding my secret. Something about this man and this moment tells me it's time to stop. Or at least tell someone so they can hold me accountable.

We sit on the cool ground and wait for our train to come. A woman's soft voice chimes above us, letting us know in both Korean and English that our train will be coming soon. I turn my head towards Michael as he holds my hand despite the heat of the subway station.

"I need to tell you something."

Michael's smile disappears and suddenly he looks worried. Concern grows in his eyes. "What is it?"

We've been dating for less than a month. I take a breath and watch the people file towards the platform. A gust of hot air passes us as the subway train on the other side comes to a complete stop.

"I have an eating disorder," I finally say. I see him take a breath. He squeezes my hand. The warm voice over the intercom informs us that the train is arriving.

"Is there anything I can do?"

I shake my head. "I don't know…I just," I pause. Our train comes to a stop and we instinctively get up. "I just needed to tell someone."

Michael nods. "Thank you for telling me. I'll help in any way I can." He squeezes my hand again and we stand in line in front of the doors, waiting to move forward.

Phase 5:
I Tried To Change But I Couldn't.

Triggers include, but aren't limited to:
- Ariana Grande

- Seeing my boyfriend look at other women
- Watching TV shows or movies with skinny or fit actresses
- Anxiety after saying idiotic things
- Seeing my body in the mirror after a shower
- Seeing my body in the reflection of the bathroom stall doors
- Seeing my reflection at all
- Stepping on to the scale to see I've gained any weight
- Stepping on the scale to see I haven't gained any weight
- Stepping on the scale
- Wearing clothes that used to fit but are now too tight
- Going up a clothing size
- Trying on clothes in a dressing room
- Fighting with my boyfriend
- My boyfriend refusing to have sex with me
- Seeing old pictures of myself
- Eating anything that isn't "healthy"
- Eating "healthy" foods in mass quantities
- Eating

Phase 6:
I Can Stop Some Of The Behaviors But Not All Of Them.

My Eating Disorder sits across the kitchen table from me with a cup of hot coffee placed between her hands. She sits up straight, crossing her legs above the knee. Everything she does looks effortless.

"Why don't you just give up white sugar and white flour again?" she says, offering suggestions at how I can finally lose the baby weight. "It worked last time when you did it with Jonah."

I shake my head, thinking back to that time almost ten years ago. Nineteen years old and engaged. I was going to university, working two jobs, and living with my alcoholic mother.

I was someone completely different.

"My life has changed," I say defensively. "I have a toddler. A partner. I cook for three." My Eating Disorder shakes her head, looking unimpressed. I continue, "I have to make food that they enjoy too. I can't just focus on me anymore."

"Even so," she says, "you sure worked out a lot more back then. You would have never let yourself get to…" she points at me, "this."

Shame fills the pit of my stomach like a fire, its embers constantly hot and glowing. The fire picks up when I think of myself now compared to my nineteen-year-old self.

"I don't have as much time now," I stutter.

She scoffs.

"Are you sure? You didn't have time back then." Her long blonde and pink hair catches the morning sunshine as she takes another sip of coffee.

"I wasn't a mom."

There is a lull in our conversation. My Eating Disorder looks around and then towards her flat stomach. She puts the cup of coffee back on the table and smooths out her black V-neck T-shirt, running her fingers over the fabric.

I look down at my own stomach. It's soft and round—the skin on it sags now. I can picture the stretch marks from my pregnancy that run from my pubic area all the way to my belly button. I have struggled to find beauty in my "mom body."

My Eating Disorder is right. I do have time. Why don't I utilize it? As I start filling in the schedule in my mind of when

I can work out and how I can meal plan for healthier options, she starts up again.

"What about counting calories? Remember, Michael said they did that in college and lost all the weight they had put on in their freshman year."

"I've tried that. I only last a day or two before I give up. It's too much. Too triggering."

She throws her head back and laughs. "*Triggering?* It should be *motivating*. Don't you want to lose weight? Don't you even care anymore?"

The fire in my stomach grows larger. It heats up my cheeks.

"I... I do. I... I just don't know how to get back to where I was." I feel my face drop. "I feel lost."

"It's because you are." She tucks her hair behind her ear, showing off a long, dangling earring. "What happened to the determined Summer I used to know?"

I turn my head and let my gaze fall to the floor. Dust bunnies lift in the breeze of the Toyo heating stove. I run my fingers through my choppy, shoulder-length bob. It's unkempt. I don't have time to style it anymore.

"I'm trying. I'm taking care of myself."

"When was the last time you even worked out regularly? When was the last time you kept a routine?" Before I can say anything, my Eating Disorder chimes in. "Remember... Remember when you were with Jonah? People said you had *so much* self-control. Now look at you. You can't even stop yourself from stuffing your face every day. You can't even find time to do a thirty-minute workout."

I can feel the tears start to form in my eyes. She's right.

"Well, I'm doing intermittent fasting again," I offer. She nods briefly. "I got down to my goal weight before I had Matilda, remember? I finally fit into my old clothes, my old Waffle Company shirt from when I was with Jonah."

"But how fast is that going to get you to where you need to go, Summer?" My Eating Disorder stands up, walks towards the window looking out at the freshly fallen snow.

She's wearing my old skinny jeans. The high-waisted ones with the frayed bottoms. She tucks her shirt into the top so you can see how thin she is. She doesn't have a "mom pooch," no fat in her lower stomach like I do. Her thighs look somehow curvy and strong, but skinny.

She turns back towards me and looks me directly in the eyes. Her arms are crossed and she says quietly, "You could do it again."

I watch her, silent, contemplating.

"No," I finally say. "I can't."

"But you *could*. You did it before and got the results you wanted. It would happen so much faster."

"I don't *need* it to. I'm doing it slowly so it stays off." My Eating Disorder walks back to the table and sits down. She frowns.

"Michael doesn't love you, you know that?"

The fire in my stomach is fully ignited. My body burns with shame.

"Yes, he does." I start to cry.

"He doesn't love your body anymore. He knows how much weight you've put on since you've started dating." I shake my head, speechless. "He thinks you're *disgusting*."

"No, no he doesn't."

"He knows you're a failure, Summer." She pauses and squints her eyes at me. "If you just had control, if you just did it again, he would love you."

I place my face in my hands and let my body shake with the sadness of her truth.

Phase 7:
I Can Stop The Behaviors, But Not My Thoughts.

I shouldn't eat anything before noon.
I should work out tonight.
I shouldn't have that cookie. Too much sugar.
I should quit alcohol. Too calorie-dense.
I shouldn't have too much peanut butter on my toast. Too many calories.
I should try to fit in more cardio.
I shouldn't say anything about my body around my daughter.
I should go back to being vegan. I lost weight that way.
I shouldn't do this.
I should do that.
I shouldn't.
I should.

Phase 8:
I Am Often Free From Behaviors And Thoughts, But Not All The Time.

I started EMDR (Eye Movement Desensitization and Reprocessing) therapy after having my child. Although I originally went to talk about my traumatic labor, my Eating Disorder reappeared. My therapist, Jocelyn, is a short, squat woman with a flare towards goth styles. She wears bright purple cat-eye glasses and sports a fresh hand tattoo. I appreciate her even more when she validates my feelings by saying phrases like, "Yeah, that fucking sucks" or "Oh my god, I can't believe you went through that." She suggests EMDR specifically since eating disorders are rooted in a fear of lack of control. Through exposure therapy and reprocessing of neural pathways, the eventual hope is that talking about the eating disorder and dealing with food will become easier.

My first session is spent placing myself in my safe space, a place in my mind I can go when the emotions and memories become overwhelming. I close my eyes and focus. I'm suddenly sitting in the kitchen of my imaginary downtown house in Juneau, Alaska. It sits on the top of Main Street, and I look out the large, white bay windows to the cool blue channel surrounded by snow-covered mountains. Fairy lights twinkle around me as I sip hot coffee and watch as the snow falls in fat flakes. It is the early morning and Michael and my daughter, Matilda, are asleep. The house is silent, calm, and quiet.

Carefully, over the course of a couple of months, Jocelyn walks me through memory after memory, always being sure to take me back to this safe spot to ground me. I'm surprised at where we go and what moments I relive.

I relive the time my father and I are at Disney World. I splash through puddles in a rainstorm, and we duck inside one of the many stores. From behind me, he suddenly says, "Man, did you hear that couple out there?"

"No? What couple?" I respond, curious.

"They were outside while you were splashing. I overheard them wondering who that chubby girl jumping in puddles was," he laughs as he says it. There must be something funny about being called fat.

I turn to look at him, shocked.

"What are you talking about? Did they really say that?" He must see the hurt in my eyes.

"I'm just *teasing*. There was nobody. I'm just *joking*."

"That's not funny," I say, frustrated, turning to leave the conversation.

"It's just a joke," he says, shaking his head.

Then there's the main memory we start with. My best friend, Sammy, and I are downtown waiting for the city bus to come by. She's brought her new friend, Jonas, one of the only out students at our school. He's mean and petty and I already hate him. They are comparing waist sizes by cupping their hands around them. They laugh when my waist isn't "small" enough to fit within my fingers.

Eventually, over time, the thoughts of food and weight and size start to become less intense, despite my postpartum body. I look forward to our sessions knowing these feelings are starting to disappear.

Phase 9:
I Am Free From Behaviors And Thoughts.

I imagine recovery as standing on a mountaintop with the summer sunshine beaming down on my freckled shoulders. It's my hand on my child's back as she wraps her arm around my strong, tanned thighs. It's wearing a sports bra and a pair of jogging shorts feeling confident in my flat stomach, no "flap" from my c-section scar.
> It's having control.
>> Of my body.
>>> Of my thoughts.
>>> Of my Eating Disorder.

But I don't imagine it as loving who I am now or loving the body I currently possess. And because of this, I worry that recovery is something of a tall tale.

Phase 10. I Am Recovered.

*Phases taken & adapted from *8 Keys to Recovery from an Eating Disorder* by Carolyn Costin and Gwen Schubert Grabb

Summer A.H. Christiansen is a writer, mother, and lifelong Alaskan residing on the unceded land of the T'aaḵu Ḵwáan and A'akw Ḵwáan. Her work has been published in *Silver Rose Magazine*, *Tidal Echoes*, *Alaska Women Speak*, and *Drizzle Review*.

Four Women Laying Domino Trains

by Alex Carrigan

After Mahogany L. Browne and Nina Simone

Four women sit around
a mahogany picnic table
for a game of Mexican trains
on a late July evening.
The domino tiles clatter
like the ice in their glasses
of iced tea as they move
their hands around and scramble them.
With the tiles divided, the game begins.

The first woman starts the train
by laying the double twelve piece.
She has spent her
life laying down ceramic pathways
for others to walk down.
She labored to put these paths down,
watching women with designer shoes
nearly step on her hands while she worked.
She imagines that drops of blood

formed by these stilettos
formed the pips on the domino,
and that's the only reason why
those women's shoes
have red bottoms.

The second woman spends most of the game
intersecting with other paths
instead of building onto her own.
She's often found it hard to pick a direction,
even unable to follow the lines
painted on the floor of the hospital
she labors away in.
Playing dominoes is asking her
to choose the gangplank
instead of the roller coaster,
so her train remains on the turntable.

The third woman coyly laughs
and giggles each time
she lays a tile down on her train.
She's managed to make it
through life grabbing people by the wrist
and taking them wherever she chooses.
None of them ever complained,
especially since she sweetly told them
what lay at the end of the path.
For her, the pips are like the
mole she paints above the corner
of the strawberry colored lips
men like to taste.

The last woman mutters obscenities under her breath
every time she draws a tile from the pile.
She's struggled the most in building paths
during this game and in life.
Her set of tiles lay on their sides
like tombstones erected in a cemetery following a war.
Her hands are calloused
like a gravedigger's,
as she often builds down instead of out.

Four women sit around
a mahogany picnic table
and continue to lay down paths for plastic trains
neither they nor anyone else
can ever take a ride on.
Once they finish,
they'll destroy those paths
and try to reconfigure them again.

Maybe the next game will
form a train line like the Yamanote,
where the domino lines
form a circle instead of spreading out
like a compass rose.
Maybe then the women
won't need directions or guidance,
and instead they can
walk carefully between the pips
to see where they end up.

'Four Women Laying Domino Trains' by Alex Carrigan originally
appeared in *Bourgeon* (July 2022).

Alex Carrigan (he/him; @carriganak) is an editor, poet, and critic from Virginia. His debut poetry chapbook, *May All Our Pain Be Champagne: A Collection of Real Housewives Twitter Poetry* (Alien Buddha Press, 2022), was longlisted for Perennial Press' 2022 Chapbook Awards. He has had fiction, poetry, and literary reviews published in *Quail Bell Magazine*, *Lambda Literary Review*, *Barrelhouse*, *Sage Cigarettes* (Best of the Net Nominee, 2023), 'Stories About Penises' (Guts Publishing, 2019), and more. He is also the co-editor of *Please Welcome to the Stage...: A Drag Literary Anthology* with House of Lobsters Literary. For more information, visit carriganak.wordpress.com.

These Ceremonies, These Rituals

by J.D. Harlock

Though she grew up on Marx
and never found God

I remember when my poor mother dragged me to that old church
hoping I would pray my heart out
and mean my every word

but the choir was a bore, the sermon a pain
and I would just stand there,
fidgeting in place, trying not to scream
as she smiled politely
and nodded her head

unbearable though it may be
it was nothing like what was to come

because these ceremonies I loathe
have altogether taken on another form

now congregated in rallies
delivered right to our homes

no longer are they the formalities
we obligate ourselves with
but rituals

upheld by our elders
and venerated by our clerics

rabid masses calling out
for someone, something
that will deliver them
unto salvation
with venerations and vigils

until everyone is honored
and nothing besides remains

because it doesn't end
and it never will
that is the point

For we once prayed to Our Lord in heaven
But now we pray to our lords on earth

J.D. Harlock is a Syrian Lebanese Palestinian writer &
editor based in Beirut. In addition to serving as editor-at-large
at *Wasifiri* and poetry editor at *Solarpunk Magazine*, he's had
his work featured in *Strange Horizons*, *Star*Line*, and the *SFWA*
Blog, among others. You can always find him on Twitter and
Instagram posting updates on his latest projects.

Trance

by Tricia Gates Brown

I SNATCH SOME FABRIC FROM the scrap basket, holding it up to the improv quilt square taking shape—'80s playlist crooning in the background, or old Lionel, the window cracked so I can hear crickets or frogs or mourning doves, depending on the season. As I quilt, I sing to my cat, who surely thinks this tidbit was written for her: "*My love, just thinking about you baby blows my mind.*" In a pandemic, with group singing silenced, this evening ritual gains currency.

Trance, I've come to call it—though for me, it's a new word. *Trance: to enter a state of profound abstraction or absorption.* According to some anthropologists, it's what we humans do—our distinguishing feature, the need for trance. Perhaps our highly discursive brains necessitate it—we need cognitive rest the same as we need all kinds of rest. The word "trance" has problematic associations, surely, conjuring images of self-appointed shamans or altered states of consciousness and glossolalia. But the fact is, we all trance out each day.

Throughout human history, group singing and chant were often our most prominent forms of formal trance. Until recent times, most cultures sang together at least weekly in spiritual services like church. At the tiny Episcopal church where I serve as ordained deacon, we resumed singing in fall 2021, all in attendance promisingly vaxxed. Singing together was wonderful... And rough. Though our parish doesn't have a song leader, we have a gifted young musician—self-taught on organ and guitar—and that first Sunday, he chose familiar hymns as I defaulted to song leader. *Morning Has Broken. Amazing Grace.* But we seemed to skip measures at the ends of choruses, and I struggled to catch up. Every first measure, clipped. Singing together purportedly has beneficial physiological effects, from stimulating the immune system to boosting relaxation to releasing the bonding hormone oxytocin. But this time, I wondered.

Especially with church attendance falling, collective singing does become more and more rare. How will we sing together? Based on the benefits, group singing is a trance we could use. Still, I understand the baggage around church singing. I often feel manipulated by it, not to mention the theology of a big-God-in-the-sky who wants nothing more than to be praised. On the other hand, I feel no less manipulated by group singing at, say, a folk concert. Yet I find this group singing moving. Why the different reactions? The problematic theology, I suppose.

For Lent 2020, I chose to delve into music. I've long resisted the idea that Lent requires subtraction or withholding, and instead see the ritual as delving deep into the roots of a thing— like a symbol of winter nourishment preceding spring's dramatic resurrection, the profusion of rebirth. I looked for ways to go deeper, and that year it was music. I made new playlists. I filled more space with deep music listening and less talk. I let music have its way with me, and ever since, I relate differently to music. Yet despite these gains, something has been lost in not sharing music with others.

Thus, I look for trance and communal singing elsewhere, such as quilting alongside Sybil, my cat. I hear snippets of song in leaf wind and the sway of cloud formations, or in the hush of the matted grass I walk over each morning rounding our hayfield, the purring of a cat. I am grateful to trance out as I do. Of course, there are ample ways to trance out with smartphones—clearly not all beneficial.

So I grab another scrap of fabric. I add it to the quilt square, singing a bit of chorus as I do. Mary Chapin Carpenter: *Now that it's twilight, twilight....* Sybil stretches her arms in approval and purrs along.

Tricia Gates Brown works as a writer and editor in Oregon's Willamette Valley, where she lives on a farm. Her essays and poetry have appeared regularly in periodicals, including *Oregon Humanities*, *Portland Magazine*, and *Rathalla Review*; and her novel *Wren* won a 2022 Independent Publishers Award Bronze Medal.

Journaling

by Linda McCauley Freeman

I pull out the old spiral notebooks
totaling all the years I could write—
my life re-lived in the time it took
to read what I scribbled each night.

Unbuttoned and undressed, I was unmuted.
I chose exposure: my mind, my day
any way and then in the only way suited—
my pen and paper unfolding what may.

I bowed daily to the troth,
unburied my long or newly dead,
wrung what I wrought, every thought,
what I did, what he or she said.

So many words splattered
across the page as if I mattered.

Across the page as if it mattered
So many words splattered—

what I did, what he or she said.
Wrung what I wrought, every thought,
unburied my long or newly dead.
I bowed daily to the troth,

my pen and paper unfolding what may,
any way and then in the only way suited—
I chose exposure: my mind, my day
unbuttoned and undressed. I was unmuted.

To read what I scribbled each night,
my life re-lived in the time it took
totaling all the years I could write—
I pull out the old spiral notebooks.

Linda McCauley Freeman is the author of the full-length poetry collection *The Family Plot* (Backroom Window Press, 2022) and has been widely published in international journals, including in a Chinese translation. She was nominated for a Pushcart Prize in 2022. Recently she was the featured poet in *The Poet Magazine*, appeared in *Delta Poetry Review*, *Amsterdam Quarterly*, and won Grand Prize in StoriArts' Maya Angelou poetry contest. She received a grant from Arts MidHudson and was selected for Poets Respond to Art 2020, 2021, and 2022 shows. She was a three-time winner in the Talespinners Short Story contest judged by Michael Korda. She has an MFA from Bennington College and is the former poet-in-residence of the Putnam Arts Council. She lives in the Hudson Valley, NY. Follow her at facebook.com/LindaMcCauleyFreeman and Twitter @LindaMccFreeman. LindaMcCauleyFreeman.com

Key to Itemizing

by Karuna Mistry

Morning
Lithuanian lady
Outside is looking shady
Have you packed an umbrella?
Also check for your postbox letters
Snap the baby in the car. She's already looking sleepy
Close the polished car door. Slam the house door. Lock. Walk
Then bolt, back. Hold. Push, no motion on the front door.
       Walk on. Wait, rewind. Repeat
Check your coat. Check your wallet. Check your phone is
       locked. Check for **keys**. Check for baby
Repeat the mental jot. Adjust the flowerpots. Pick up and
       place back on the same slot
For the sixth time—trace round on your house plot
You've not even left the bloody spot!
Lady, are you losing the plot?
Check this. Check that
Repeat until crazy
Quirky surprise
You're not
Czech

Karuna Mistry is a British writer of Indian ethnicity. His work can be found in various poetry anthologies including *McKinley Publishing Hub*, *Open Door*, and *Sweetycat Press*. As well as poetry, drawing, and blogging, his creativity includes magazine editorship, photography, and design—his occupation by day is higher education marketing. Karuna is currently working on his debut poetry book. @karunamistrypoetry
karunacreations.wordpress.com

New Roommate

by Mark Thomas

I sighed and catalogued the changes.

A padded wing chair had left,
and four disc-like depressions,
carpet crop circles,
marked the place where the alien chair
first landed.

Six framed pictures had fled,
leaving a pattern of faded squares
on the living room plaster,
as if the sun were a burglar
who loved Mondrian.

Gaps in the book case;
evidence of enterprising volumes
who tunneled to freedom.

A kitchen clock skedaddled,
its familiar sound replaced by a dripping tap.
Colourful curtains once hung by their fingertips
from that window.
But they've let go,
fluttered to the sidewalk, and billowed away.

Now, outside, footsteps swell and diminish,
full of deceptive approaches and false retreats,
a reminder that one careless moment
is all it takes.

A sentry nods, defences are lowered like eyelids,
a gate is unbolted; heart-shaped portcullis left ajar.

That's all it takes for one to scramble out
and another, smelling of bleach and loneliness,
to sneak in.

Mark Thomas is a retired English and Philosophy teacher
and ex-member of Canada's national rowing team.

Off God

by Valerie Anne Burns

THE ONLY AUTHENTIC CONNECTION to divinity I feel is when standing under my hummingbird feeder, hearing and feeling the vibration of their translucent wings. Each wondrous being bursts with vibrant color and fierceness, possesses a determination to make its way in the world with grace. When they fly around me, I feel them grazing my hair and shoulder as they scan my energy. They hover and stare directly into my eyes. I've come to ask these near-weightless creatures to heal me. I feel privileged to be in their presence as they gather sweet nectar, to make their lives a little easier on a parched Earth that now provides for them far fewer blooms than it used to.

On evenings after long days of doctor appointments, while feeling a swell of anxiety, I'd seek the thread of peace and ritual that my spirit stretched far for. I'd look through the canyon, over the old Mission's terra cotta steeples, to the dusty-blue ocean as the sun closed another day. Many evenings, I observed the most extraordinary salmon-colored clouds. I imagined that my beloved Van Gogh acknowledged me by painting the expansive sky in colors only he could copy. In these quiet glimpses into the natural world, I silently made a wish to be free of whatever bound me.

For decades, I was on a devoted, spiritual path. I'd been involved in everything from *A Course in Miracles* to attendance at the Unity church, affirmations, praying, and full-on daily devotion. Since being back in Santa Barbara, I took a spiritual U-turn when breast cancer knocked at my door.

It happened fast.

The moment the diagnosis hit, all my spiritual work disappeared in a cyclone of shock and betrayal. I'd been wholly focused on finding a tailor-made purpose where my talents would be fully utilized—where I'd be in vibrant health, receive the prosperity that always eluded me, and just like in the movies, find ideal love. Why not? I knew it was time to transcend all the difficulty.

Instead, the gods in all their humor, wisdom, and ironies blindsided me with The Big C.

I couldn't squash the inherited gene from my mother. I'd been following all the holistic guidelines and a mélange of gurus to keep it at bay. Plus, I was juicing organic beets, carrots, and extreme greens. It felt inconceivable that I'd be presented with one more heavy burden. I already felt like I was in a small boat where my hands clutched the sides, unable to withstand an additional strike, a torrential storm that could sink me for good.

This unstable boat let me row to a sea of consternation. When I was suffering from cancer, infections, and surgeries, the bills didn't conveniently stop. My need for security and reliable support was critical.

Close to this span of time, two men who were deeply close to me (former lovers and always friends) died at an age far too young, the ritual of meeting for espresso and sharing barbs lost forever. Selfishly, I needed them more than ever and resented their act of disappearing from my orbit. Their deaths opened a fresh wound of loss in my life.

Both men brought me a kind of ease and fulfillment—they understood my quirks, my sassy nature. I'd heard the word "joy" mentioned quite a bit amongst the people I'd met who walked on enlightened paths. Then I wondered about my love of cynical or sarcastic humor to navigate life. I gravitated toward people with an appreciation of humor; those who could land it like a blade, who caused me to throw my head back in a rousing laughter. I'd had great laughs with both men. In my darkest and diciest of times, sharp humor was the balm that soothed me on unexpected rough roads. I wasn't prepared for how relentlessly harsh the road would be. Everything I was working on to create this new joyful life seemed to blow away with the Santa Ana winds.

When the nurse practitioner's number came up on my cell phone on that fateful day, I knew from the soft tone in her voice. It was bad news.

I felt betrayed by God and my commitment to spirituality.

Enough was enough. I discontinued everything I'd been doing and chose another way. This new direction included my connection to nature and beauty. I binged on my favorite black-and-white drama and romance movies from the 1930s and 1940s. I also lost myself in the longest cable series I could find, *Mad Men*, *Downton Abbey*, and *Sex and the City*. These entertainments were antidotes to the mind-numbing medical info I was managing.

At night, instead of listening to calming meditation music specifically designed for patients like me, I went to my hand-selected music on Pandora. This playlist was an assemblage of passionate music—from opera to Adele.

Escape was my answer. Personally, I thought denial would be quite useful. I ate a lot more dark chocolate.

Since I received the opposite of what I'd been envisioning and praying for, I came home from an appointment discussing my diagnosis, walked out to the porch, and shouted to the mountain peak, "That's it. I'm off God!"

Relief flowed over me like a waterfall. I'd spent so much time meditating and affirming when I was "on God," it was comforting to put it all aside. I contemplated what I would fill that particular free time with.

A couple of months passed while I was following this revelation, and I came to realize that without thinking about it, I had found the most comfort in standing still. I found this quote by Henry Miller to be quite significant: "Either you take in believing in miracles or you stand still like the hummingbird."

All human beings have their struggles. I'd had a full dose since I came into this spinning ocean of emptiness as a tiny being in Miami, only to lose my mother three years later to breast cancer. I continued to wonder about the spiritual concept of being here on Earth for a divine purpose—following my bliss—but despair shrouded me. With a belief that there's a divine intelligence, something greater than me that has the capacity to create perfection in nature, wouldn't it also see me as a particle of perfection?

Would my life be spared?

When I'd heard people speak about a continual sense of being guided by God, or having heard angels guide their destiny, I felt skepticism and envy. I can't say that I've ever experienced that type of mystical guidance. For all the times I'd stated, "Show me the way," or, "How can I best serve?" or "What is my true purpose?" I never heard or saw a direct comeback, sign, or answer. Where was that still small voice? I'd felt slighted because I so wanted to feel God the omniscient, or see a supernatural vision of some kind to justify my craggy life path.

As a visual and instinctual person by nature, I never understood why I wasn't seeing the Virgin Mary in my dreams, or an angel appear in the foam of a cappuccino. I've had tens of thousands of cappuccinos in my lifetime, beginning in Rome—a popular place for paranormal sightings—when I was nineteen and truly open.

I'd lost so many loved ones, including parents, grandparents, and friends at an early age, that it seemed natural to be guided and held in a warm embrace by them. I couldn't imagine the friends who'd recently died not participating in directing my life from some distant star. I'd call out to all those I'd lost, at 3:00 a.m., when my mind was racing on insomnia, down roads of insecurity, and leaping onto other trains of spiraling thought. It usually took me until 6:00 in the morning to quiet down enough to fall back into one or two more hours of sweet sleep.

As I began a journey on the medical path, like a soldier marching from one appointment to the next, one surgery to the next, I was thrown into a surreal environment. I'd enter dull hallways and offices painted in colors I'd never come across in my decorating hunts. The times I sat on a table waiting for the doctor to come in, staring at dreary green, blinding white, or beige walls were more than I care to count. Where did they find those colors? Was there a paint color palette made for medical facilities only? I could see the label saying, "For hospital and medical professional offices only. Guaranteed to make your patient more depressed and sicker than they already are." It was only the beginning of the hell I was to embark on, as if a spooky ship from *Pirates of the Caribbean* forced me to board and took me to dark, cobweb-filled waterways. This was the daily rut that went on and on. There was nothing enlightening about it.

In those dreary hallways, divine beauty fell away. Everything sad blended together in that first month of appointments, blood work, and tests that involved needles and machines. All of this I experienced in the same scratchy blue-and-white gowns.

The appointments were all within a six-block radius near the hospital, and I would far too often find myself in the parking lot of one of the six doctors when I was meant to be in the parking lot of another. Autopilot. The car seemed to drive itself while I was altogether somewhere else, dreaming of a boat with white sails that took me to clear water, blue as a pristine swimming pool.

Physical pain appeared as permanent foe. I went from operating rooms to my bedroom where tubes with bulbous drains hung from me as if they belonged. I was in a place far separated from any realm where God, angels, guides, or even friendly ghosts spent time together.

It threw me into cursing like I never had before. I was cursing the pain and humiliation of a long, harsh path—even longer than the doctors could've anticipated. I felt I had earned a new freedom to curse. I cursed from pain, and from running to its opposite of paralyzed silence that only my sofa could hold. I cursed the interruption of my life and hopes. The thought of romance ever entering my life again seemed as hopeless as if I were shredding it with my bare hands.

Who'd want a mangled, scarred woman in her late fifties?

I needed answers, but none showed up in my cappuccinos or under my pillow. I don't recall asking to be in a place of surrender, but that is exactly where I landed. It's not as if

I made a conscious choice. While on the path of threat—a threat to my very life—the only thing to do was surrender. Because of both threat and surrender, I existed in a vastly unique way. What I did manage to do were effortless spiritual rituals that kept me sane and safe.

I'd sip tea as early morning unfolded, visiting the magic of my angelic hummingbirds that trusted me enough to take nectar from my hand. I'd observe how they moved through their day with an inimitable energy, surviving whatever challenges might be put before them. As evening's light drifted to my door, I'd sit to take in the sunset, noticing a deeper shade of pink and orange that reminded me of a creamsicle. The freshly painted clouds would easily float by while deepening to a burnt-cinnamon red as the sun sank on another day. I was still alive, most likely by divine guidance. The temperature would then drop in the final glow of light, and I'd ponder the idea that this was my life, and it was all there was in that very moment.

As an emerging writer, **Valerie Anne Burns** is excited to have "Flying Nighties" from *Caution: Mermaid Crossing, Voyages of a Motherless Daughter*, included in *Chicken Soup for the Soul: Tough Times Won't Last but Tough People Will*, released November 2nd, 2021. She's had two essays published in *HerStry Literary Magazine*: "Venice Vision" in September 2020 and "Your Bed" May 2021. *Libretto Magazine* published "He's on Top of the World and I'm Not" June 2021. In September 2021, she received a Finalist Award from Page Turner Awards in the category of manuscript submission. Valerie Anne was awarded scholarships to the 2019 Santa Barbara Writers Conference and the 2016 Prague Summer Writing Program. In addition, she was sponsored on a trip to Italy and the Dominican Republic for a breast cancer survivor retreat, where an essay from her book became a launching point for the workshop presented, "Living and Healing Through Color." She journeyed to Rome in September 2022 for the same nonprofit where she blogged about her experience as the 1st International Freestyle survivor participant. She previously worked in Hollywood as a story editor and in production, as well as having her own business as a makeover specialist for home décor and wardrobe. Santa Barbara is home, and the place where Valerie Anne has survived breast cancer. Being near the ocean brings out her "inner mermaid" and gives her the peace and clarity she needs to write, along with the strength and grace she needs to mother herself through the stormiest weather.

Myth of Origin

by Toti O'Brien

Small saucepan simmering on the stove,
just one and the sauce is always the same
but perfect, but just so. The fish comes
into the sauce on special occasions
only to celebrate, to escalate abundance
with its bounty of salt, oil. Phosphorus,
calcium, but that she wouldn't know.

Tea served in tall glasses. Don't ask her
to bring out the china, the silver spoons.
Cold tea is kept in the fridge in a bottle,
loaded with sugar and lemon, the color
of amber, sweeter than ambrosia and
tastier than liquor. She pours.
Don't ask her for napkins.

The tray of almond cookies from the
patisserie her son likes, for her son to
bring home each time he comes to visit.
First, a lunch of pasta with fish sauce
served at the unclothed kitchen table.
The intoxicating smells of oregano
and basil.

Then her son naps in his childhood
room, the bed freshly made, the scent
of detergent. Time to leave. Do not
forget the cookies, hard under
your teeth, but exquisite mix of spices
and nuts. Large tray for the road
and for the grandchildren.

She waves him goodbye from the porch
bedecked with peppers and garlic. How
did repetition become. A song. One of each,
pot, sauce, tea, goodbye, batch of cookies.
Tiny loops, like safety pins securing her apron
like the circlets marking those dates
on the calendar hung to the kitchen wall.

Originally published in California Quarterly, Vol 48.2

Toti O'Brien is the Italian Accordionist with the Irish last
name. Born in Rome, living in Los Angeles, she is an art-
ist, musician and dancer. She is the author of *Other Maidens*
(BlazeVOX, 2020), *An Alphabet of Birds* (Moonrise Press, 2020),
In Her Terms (Cholla Needles Press, 2021), *Pages of a Broken Di-
ary* (Pski's Porch, 2022), and *Alter Alter* (Elyssar Press, 2022).

A Life of Index Cards

by J. J. Steinfeld

A man of remarkable precision
put his mistakes, physical and financial,
on 3-by-5 index cards
dated, labelled, and numbered,
neat upper-case printing, red ink,
starting as an exuberant lad of fifteen
now a circumspect man of fifty
believes there is both wonder
and beauty in the precision
his opinion not changing
day after day
month after month
year after year
even as the price
of index cards increased
and their quality, in his opinion,
decreased
then an arsonist
burns down his apartment house
(wrong building, street number reversed,
but that's another story of imprecision)
all his possessions, all his savings,
except the index-card file boxes

taken by the imprecise flames.
Thank God, the man of remarkable precision thinks,
prints out on a 3-by-5 index card
FORGOT TO RENEW FIRE INSURANCE
dates, labels, and numbers his latest mistake
in control of his life again.

Poet, fiction writer, and playwright **J. J. Steinfeld** lives on Prince Edward Island, where he is patiently waiting for Godot's arrival and a phone call from Kafka. While waiting, he has published 23 books, including *An Unauthorized Biography of Being* (Stories, Ekstasis Editions, 2016), *Absurdity, Woe Is Me, Glory Be* (Poetry, Guernica Editions, 2017), *A Visit to the Kafka Café* (Poetry, Ekstasis Editions, 2018), *Gregor Samsa Was Never in The Beatles* (Stories, Ekstasis Editions, 2019), *Morning Bafflement and Timeless Puzzlement* (Poetry, Ekstasis Editions, 2020), *Somewhat Absurd, Somehow Existential* (Poetry, Guernica Editions, 2021), and *Acting on the Island* (Stories, Pottersfield Press, 2022).

Honeysuckle Reflections

by Lauren Wester

I FOLLOWED HIM TO THE FOREST'S EDGE—running to keep up with his older, longer strides. Tendrils of frizzy hair swirled around my face, and I, with my chubby hands, tried to beat back the tickling strands being thrown about by unwelcome gusts of wind. I kept my eyes on our feet, following the familiar path from back door to fence line, marveling at the freshly mown grass, plush between my bare toes. A fresh gust of wind came from a new direction, clearing the hair from my eyes and bringing with it a new scent. A sweet scent that pulled my gaze up. There, behind my brother, who was already plucking color from the edge, was a wall of yellow and white flowers dotting what—just the day before—had been a plethora of green leaves twined together.

"Here!" He spun around, two tiny flowers in his hand— one yellow, one white. He held his palm out, eager for me to take one. So I did. White, because it matched my outfit. And he showed me how to pinch the bottom and pull out the stem holding a miniscule amount of sweet liquid that would become a touchstone signaling warmer weather and outdoor adventures.

Some twenty-odd years later, as I walked from the back door of my own home down to the freshly tilled garden, the scent hit me again, and I found myself running back to the forest's edge. I found the white flowers covering the green wall and instinctively grinned. I reached out and plucked a flower from the vines, rolled it gently between my fingers, and inhaled the sweet aroma before following the steps that had become second nature after two decades of repetition.

Pinch. Pull. Savor.

That singular, honeysuckle scent has followed me from spring to spring, ushering in a new season and returning to me a sense of home that is bound uniquely to nature. It is not an anomaly, this seasonal awakening of the senses. Each year it dawns, marking the passage of time in a way that our calendars and clocks will never be able to emulate.

Lauren Wester grew up in the southern United States surrounded by family, good food, and a house full of books. Her love for literature began at a young age and has held her captive ever since. She believes in the power of putting pen to paper and using her words to positively impact her readers.

Lauren holds a bachelor's degree in English and has worked as a journalist, social media director, and now marketing specialist. When she isn't at work, she can be found haunting bookstores, revelling in coffee shops, and enjoying the company of her husband and two cuddly dogs.

Waltz for a Hawk

by Brianna Cunliffe

once I knew a boy who could spool an owl's call
like strange grey honey
from the back of his throat

he took us looking for killers under bruising crimson sky
black-back gulls, hawks, adolescent eagles
he took offerings. lens caps, yellow notebooks.
the carcass of last night's chicken

we took nothing. we held our breath
as he held up a fist in the low forest by the island's end
and we ceased, every creature, all the chickadees quivering
on branches,
an unnatural night silence. he pointed, one long knobbled finger
to the hooded bird glaring into the slate sea.

a merlin, he said
the birds still as glass about to shatter
she's why they're all afraid

we were, too
cracking under the eye of that creature carved
for this cold island sky.

he told us in distracted raptures under the drumming roof
how birds' calls are fragile things, really,
how once a mountain ridge's jagged edge severed a language
and sparrows on either side became strangers to one another
after that first and great forgetting
they no longer shared a single note of song

the woodstove spat and the coals wrung out into wings
why it is that flight burns like this within us
a joy that tears the horizon from its bones
this hunger that leaves us,
land-bound

Brianna Cunliffe is an environmental justice activist and storyteller. As a queer woman who grew up on a rising shoreline, her work is animated by fierce love of the fragile places we call home. Her poems and short stories have been published in *Reckoning, Lucent Dreaming, Storm Cellar, Claw and Blossom, Blind Corner, the Poetica Review,* and more.

Pomegranate   Persephone

by Eileen Dolan

Every full rotation   come
school come floating leaves come
Monarchs' migration

at first pomegranate sighting   most
ripe most round   usually when most
needing close closeness

and the accompanying   necessary
nursing of the family soul
we gathered

around our table   shared
seeds shared a very old story shared
wonder about seasons'

traditions   So strange what holds
on   is held dear   holds
us to family—

now   the children suggest
we continue our tribute   across miles
across time

continue   the
wonder about seasons
continue
honoring the ubi sunt

Eileen Dolan is a poet writing from Austin, TX. Her work has appeared or is forthcoming in *Minerva, Vol 8; oddball magazine's St Patrick's Day Parade of Poets edition*, and *Rumors Secrets & Lies* by Anhinga Press. She also contributed a two dimensional Word Sculpture for the 2020 online Global Art Project, *Telephone*. Eileen organized and produced two two-woman shows, *Surface Tension* and *It Takes Two*, and is currently organizing another upcoming two-woman show. She received an MFA from Texas State University and has also been a practicing Medical Massage Therapist specializing in Chronic Pain for 22 years.

About the Editor

Brina Patel is a freelance writer based in Sacramento, California. Her work has been published, or is forthcoming in, *Brown Girl Magazine*, *The Mighty*, *LEVITATE Magazine*, and *Better Humans*. When she's not putting words to the page, you'll find her hiking near her Northern California home, curling up with a tear-jerking memoir, or spoiling her sassy Maltese.